Enduring Culture

A Century of Photography

OF THE SOUTHWEST INDIANS

Enduring Culture

A Century of Photography

OF THE SOUTHWEST INDIANS

By M.K. Keegan & Frontier Photographers

Wesley Bradfield, Edward S. Curtis, Wyatt Davis, Burton Frasher, Odd Halseth, John K. Hillers,
Charles Lummis, T. Harmon Parkhurst, George H. Pepper, Simeon Schwemberger,
Matilda Coxe Stevenson, J. R. Willis, Ben Wittick & Adam Clark Vroman

Foreword by N. Scott Momaday

CLEAR LIGHT PUBLISHERS, SANTA FE

ACKNOWLEDGEMENTS

I wish to thank all the following individuals and institutions with whose help and cooperation this book was made possible.

The friends and families I have photographed that are pictured in this book: the J.D. Roybal family, the Peter Garcia family, the Naranjo family, the Darrell Martinez family, the Frank Romero family, Lucy Martinez, Leandro Bernal, Rosemary Cordova, Shirley Lujan, Christine and Bernadette Eustace, Agnes Dill, and Pablita Velarde.

Richard Rudisill, Curator of Photographic History, and Arthur Olivas, Photographic Archivist, both of the Museum of New Mexico, Santa Fe, for their interest in my work from the earliest days and for their cooperation and advice throughout the many stages of the preparation of this book.

The directors and staffs of the following museums for the use of the vintage photographs in their files: The Library of Congress, The Museum of the American Indian, The Smithsonian Institution, The Seaver Center for Western History Research, The Natural History Museum of Los Angeles County, and The Southwest Museum.

My friends and professional associates for their interest in my work and their contributions to this book: Irwing Warhaftig, Eleanor Caponigro, Howard Bryan, Leon Roybal, John Dillon Fillmore, Bud Wescott, Ann Mason, and Ken Liberman.

Lou Hamlin for her friendship and generous support.

The Professional Photography Division of Eastman Kodak Company for their grant in support of the publication of this book.

A special thanks to Valerie M. Shepherd who assisted in editing: to N. Scott Momaday, who wrote the foreword; and to my husband, Harmon Houghton, for his love and support.

M.K. Keegan
Santa Fe, N.M.

First Edition, Second Printing

The text of this book was set in Bodoni by Casa Sin Nombre, Santa Fe, New Mexico. The book was printed and bound in Hong Kong by Book Art Inc., Toronto, Canada.

Traditional Native Americans believe that all of one's actions and decisions should be governed by the effects they will have on the Seventh Generation.

This book is dedicated
to the Seventh Generation

FOREWORD
by N. Scott Momaday

The wonderful thing about this book is that it plays on the seams of time.

The photographs are some of the best that have ever been taken of the American Indian, photographs taken by such masters as Edward S. Curtis, Charles Lummis, Matilda Coxe Stevenson, George H. Pepper, and T. Harmon Parkhurst. These frontier photographers worked at a time when the culture of the Indian was apparently coming to its end. Surely the photographers themselves, and those contemporaries who were fortunate enough to behold and study their work, believed that they were witnessing a culture not only in decline but indeed on the verge of extinction.

And when I say that these photographs are some of the best that have ever been taken of the American Indian, I do not exclude those by M.K. Keegan, who succeeds the frontier photographers by a hundred years, more or less. This is a considerable irony and one that must not be lost upon us. Her photographs are breathtaking reflections of the earlier work. And yet they are entirely original and unique. They are the best record we have of the strength and persistence of American Indian culture. To see these images juxtaposed is to understand something about the endurance of culture and spirit and human being. *Enduring Culture* is a title entirely fortunate and appropriate. Here is a book that teaches us something about patience and survival.

It was, I believe, in 1976 that I first met M.K. Keegan. I had gone with my children to take part in the Gourd Dance. The Kiowa Gourd Dance Society is a very old soldier society in the Kiowa tribe, and I became a member in 1969. It was a particular honor to participate in the annual dance on July 4, 1976, the 200th birthday of American independence—another irony, it would seem, since the Kiowas, along with other tribes on the Great Plains, had opposed the inexorable advance of the American soldiers upon the frontier. But at last the Plains tribes (and by and large all Indian peoples) fitted themselves into the larger pattern of patriotism, and the American Indian is among the most patriotic of Americans.

What I am getting at is this: the Fourth of July, 1976, at Carnegie, Oklahoma, was for me a celebration of Creation and belonging at the center of the world. What color and excitement and patriotism and love of earth and of what it has given to us, regardless of our racial or cultural definitions! And I have Marcia Keegan's brilliant record of this extraordinary day in my life.

Thanksgiving for such moments, and thanksgiving for this remarkable celebration of enduring culture. Not only Native Americans but all Americans ought to look deeply into this beautiful record of survival. It reminds us that we are human beings and that our destiny is to prevail over all adversities.

INTRODUCTION
by M.K. Keegan

In 1896, when the photographer Edward S. Curtis began his monumental project to document all the remaining North American Indian peoples, he believed that he was preserving a record of a vanishing culture. Curtis was by no means the only early photographer to be so moved. Though his achievement is the best-known and most comprehensive, others, too, recorded turn-of-the century Native American life, and many of their photographs deserve to be much better known. Some excellent early photographers of Southwestern Indians include the Franciscan Brother Simeon Schwemberger, the anthropologist and translator Matilda Coxe Stevenson, and the "amateur" artist Adam Clark Vroman—just three among many who devoted time and talent to preserving a way of life they believed was fascinating—and endangered.

Native cultures and peoples have undergone enormous changes since the beginning of the twentieth century. I was born in Oklahoma, the setting for some of the most visible and wrenching transformations inflicted on Native Americans by the foreigners who settled on their land. When I later moved to New Mexico and began, in 1959, to get to know and photograph the Pueblo and Navajo Indians, I was keenly aware of this history of cultural devastation, and of the changes I had witnessed in Oklahoma. Though I rejoiced in seeing the intact ancient ceremonial and daily life of the Indians of New Mexico and Arizona, I wondered how much longer it could endure. Moved by its depth and beauty, I was eager to record it for posterity. Like Curtis, I often thought that what I was seeing and recording might soon vanish.

Like Curtis, I was wrong—happily, fortunately, wrong. The essence of the Native American way of life has now proved more durable than Curtis imagined or than I first dared dream. Nowhere in the United States is this more noticeable than in the Southwest. After nearly thirty years of documenting the traditional life of the Navajo and Pueblo Indians of the Southwest, I can report that what I have witnessed in this time is not a dissolution, but a rejuvenation.

I became aware of this phenomenon during a career of publishing five books and innumerable articles on the Southwestern Indians. With the hope of understanding this phenomenon, I recently looked through Curtis's work again, and began to research the work of other early photographers, including those mentioned above. As I examined their pictures, I compared the content of their images with my own photographs, collected during twenty-five years' time. It was startling to see the similarities between my photographs and these much older pictures I had never seen before. By following my own inclination, I had photographed, in the 1960s, 1970s, and 1980s, scenes and events of Indian life that I now realized were scarcely changed from those of a hundred years earlier. More than any words, the coincidental resemblances of these images provide visible proof of the endurance of Southwestern Indian cultures.

These ageless images seem to support my personal conviction that the traditional Southwestern Indian culture has not only survived, but is actually growing stronger. In 1900, there were only eight thousand Indians on all the nineteen pueblos; there are now more than forty thousand. The population of Pojoaque Pueblo had sunk to seven by 1930, and it really did seem to be on the verge of extinction. By 1965, however, it had increased significantly, with seventy Indians living there. In Arizona, changes in the Hopi population show a similar pattern. The Hopi were numbered at slightly more than two thousand in the 1920s; their current population is four times that. These changes are evident to anyone visiting the pueblos over a long period of time, for participation in tribal activities has certainly increased during the years I have been observing them.

I offer some impressions, as anecdotal evidence:

Twenty-five years ago there were few Indian dancers, and most of them were older people. I was concerned that when these people died, the dances would end. But there has been a revival; every year there seem to be more dancers. Last year there were over six hundred dancers at Santo Domingo Pueblo. The young people have come back, and now the dancers range in age from three to eighty.

Traditional crafts like jewelry making and pottery, which once were practiced only for private domestic consumption, have attracted international attention. An appreciative public has provided a worldwide market, and Pueblo potters who formerly might have expended their talents in utilitarian work have risen to the challenge, producing pottery that is superlative in artistry and craftsmanship. Jewelers have learned to adapt traditional designs to a wider range of stones, and have allowed the ancient motifs to evolve naturally in a wide range of expressive styles. Many daily activities, such as food preparation (baking bread in the traditional horno) and home building with fresh adobe, are still practiced in time-honored ways—not for sentimental reasons, but because people still find them practical and satisfying.

The rituals of the Pueblo Indians follow the same lunar calendar they have for hundreds of years. Such continuity of custom found among the nineteen pueblos in New Mexico and the Hopi in Arizona is remarkable in American history. One explanation for this continuity may be the fact that these people are living on the same land that they have inhabited for centuries. Their strong central social organizations endured because they were never forcibly relocated. Another reason for this continuity is the relative religious freedom permitted in New Mexico. Pueblo and Navajo Indians were able to maintain their religious beliefs because, unlike states like Oklahoma, New Mexico did not enact laws banning specific Indian beliefs and practices.

This is not to say that the Southwestern Indians are living today exactly as they did one hundred years ago. Christianity has long been a part of their lives, and modern technology has been embraced with as much fervor here as anywhere in the United States. My photographs do not show the microwave ovens which speed-cook the corn stew, nor the computers Pueblo businessmen and women use to maintain their records of pottery shipped and invoices outstanding. It is not that these things do not exist. They do, but they have been assimilated into the Indians' cultural heritage in a manner that the rest of us (the dislocated African-, Asian-, and European-American newcomers) find difficult to imagine. We, the recent immigrants to their native land, embrace, instead, the typically "American" values of novelty, change, and technological innovation as the substance of our lives. The traditional Indians are perfectly happy to adapt a recent innovation if it is useful—as an adjunct to a way of life based on eternal verities. From the beginning of my acquaintance with them, it was the Indians' confidence in and attunement to the eternal verities that inspired my wonder and admiration. Thus it became my enduring commitment to try to experience, imagine, and document that more elusive subject, the traditional Indian way of life.

In this sense, too, my work is similar to the work of Curtis, who also focused on aspects of traditional Indian culture. When a modern element intruded into a picture, he cropped it out; an Indian wearing blue jeans might have been asked to change to traditional dress— sometimes even provided by Curtis himself! Though I have never gone that far, I can appreciate Curtis's choice to pose his subjects. Native Americans in his day believed—just as traditional Indians do today—that something is stolen from them when their pictures are taken. A moment's reflection will reveal that this is not merely a "primitive" notion. Any photograph of a person made without permission is an invasion of privacy; at the very least, the power of assent has been stolen from its subject. For this reason, I, too, posed my subjects, giving them the opportunity to willingly, consciously participate in the making of documents about themselves.

Over the years since I began photographing Southwestern Indians, I have had the opportunity to get to know many Pueblo and Navajo families, and have photographed the same families for four generations. During these years of attending family events and ceremonies and participating in daily life, I have been included in many personal dramas and tender, intimate moments—which I would not dream of photographically invading. They are moments to treasure, not to expose to the public. Similarly, though I have been privileged to witness some dances and rituals usually closed to non-Indians, I would no more dream of photographing private rites than I would think of stealing a church crucifix—and I would be the first to break the camera of anyone else who tried!

What moves me to such a state of reverence is not simply a conservative or old-fashioned turn of mind—it is a first-hand appreciation for the power of the living esoteric reality that informs the lives of the Southwestern Indians. The old customs retain such a grip on the people because these customs ground their lives and give them meaning. Modern man searches with restless anxiety for meaning in his existence, trying to buy it, woo it, conquer it, compete for it—to no avail. The traditional Indian life is a continuum of meaning, renewed through every daily activity. By properly performing the roles of male and female child and adult, and by executing large and small rituals, the Southwestern Indians continually affirm their relation to the rest of Nature and their place in the universe.

Modern man has much to learn from the Southwestern Indians. Curtis knew this; so did the other early photographers whose work appears in this book. It is this that makes these photographs speak to us now.

An image of a woman combing her hair with a yucca brush or stooping by the water at Acoma Pueblo evokes something timeless about ways of nurturing, and about the means of survival. In their dances, Southwestern Indians participate in Nature's regenerative power. To anyone who would demand factual proof of the power of these dances, I would say: Since I began going to Indian ceremonies in 1958, I have never been to a dance at which it did not rain or sleet or snow, either during the dance or a short time after it.

To dance during rain or snow is considered a blessing of Father Sky. The dance is like a conduit through which the energies of Nature may be channeled in order to obtain a balance between Earth and Sky. The drum is like the heartbeat of the Earth. Experiencing the dance transports both dancer and observer. In the beginning, when I watched my friends take part in the dance, I wondered why, after the dance began, they would not acknowledge me. Now I know that the dancer takes on the spirit of the animal or the cloud or the corn which is portrayed. The dancer is in a mystically receptive state in which he or she focusses on receiving the power and essence of a particular spirit. During the dance, the dancer receives the power of natural phenomena and embodies that phenomena.

The chants or prayers that accompany the ceremonies powerfully communicate the essence of Indian religion better than any prose description:

> *Oh our Mother the Earth, Oh our Father the Sky,*
> *Your children are we, and with tired backs*
> *We bring you the gifts that you love.*
> *Then weave for us a garment of brightness;*

May the warp be the white light of morning,
May the weft be the red light of evening,
May the fringes be the falling rain,
May the border be the standing rainbow.

Thus weave for us a garment of brightness
That we may walk fittingly where birds sing,
That we may walk fittingly where grass is green,
Oh our Mother the Earth, Oh our Father the Sky.

Modern man might well make such a plea to any divinity he can imagine, taking a lesson from the Southwestern Indians. Living in an area of sparse rainfall, the Indians developed a fine attunement to Nature that allowed them to survive well on minute amounts of water; it was a perfect integration of spiritual intuition and practical application. By studying these peoples' attunement to the spirit forces of the Earth, the rest of us may learn how to hold in check the dangers that threaten to annihilate our planet. The more deeply we look at the culture of our Southwestern Indians, the more evident it becomes that this way of life is not only enduring and vital, but may actually hold the keys to the survival of the human race.

1. *Canyon de Chelly*, 1904, Edward S. Curtis

2. *Canyon de Chelly*, 1972, M. K. Keegan

3. *Laguna Pueblo*, 1885, Ben Wittick

4. *Laguna Pueblo*, 1972, M. K. Keegan

5. *Acoma Woman at Waterhole*, 1904, Edward S. Curtis

6. *Acoma Woman at Waterhole*, 1970, M. K. Keegan

7. *Caroline Trujillo, Cochiti Pueblo*, 1920, T. Harmon Parkhurst

8. *Trina Encino from Acoma Pueblo*, 1974, M. K. Keegan

9. *Zuni Pueblo*, 1903, Edward S. Curtis

10. *Taos Pueblo*, 1969, M. K. Keegan

11. *Corn Dance, Jemez Pueblo*, 1908, Simeon Schwemberger

12. *Corn Dance, Santa Clara Pueblo*, 1986, M. K. Keegan

13. *Hopi Girl*, 1904, Edward S. Curtis

14. *Hopi Girl*, 1987, M. K. Keegan

15. *Man from Taos Pueblo*, 1935, T. Harmon Parkhurst

16. *Frank C. Romero from Taos Pueblo*, 1970, M. K. Keegan

17. *Buffalo Herd*, 1905, Edward S. Curtis

18. *Buffalo Herd, Taos Pueblo*, 1970, M. K. Keegan

19. *Buffalo Dancers, Tesuque Pueblo*, 1925, Edward S. Curtis

20. *Buffalo Dancers, Nambe Pueblo,* 1969, M. K. Keegan

21. *Buffalo Dance, San Ildefonso Pueblo*, 1920, Wesley Bradfield

22. *Buffalo dance, San Ildefonso Pueblo,*, 1973, M. K. Keegan

23. *Dancer with Tablita*, 1905, Edward S. Curtis

24. *Bernice Roybal from San Ildefonso Pueblo*, 1980, M. K. Keegan

25. *Acoma Pueblo*, date unknown, Wyatt Davis

26. *Acoma Pueblo*, 1972, M. K. Keegan

27. *Making Pottery, Santa Clara Pueblo,* 1920, Burton Frasher

28. *Lucy Martinez, San Ildefonso Pueblo*, 1972, M. K. Keegan

29. *The Estufa, San Ildefonso Pueblo*, 1905, Edward S. Curtis

30. *Dancers Entering Kiva, Nambe Pueblo*, 1971, M. K. Keegan

31. *Estufa, San Ildefonso Pueblo,* 1904, George H. Pepper

32. *Bernice at Kiva, San Ildefonso Pueblo*, 1971, M. K. Keegan

33. *Eagle Dance, Cochiti Pueblo*, 1935, T. Harmon Parkhurst

34. *Eagle Dance, Laguna Pueblo*, 1970, M. K. Keegan

35. *Little Daylight*, 1905, Edward S. Curtis

36. *Kiowa Boy,* 1978, M. K. Keegan

37. *Hopi Basket Maker,* 1901, Adam Clark Vroman

38. *Navajo Basket Makers*, 1970, M. K. Keegan

39. *Mrs. Yaweya Baking Bread in Horno, Laguna Pueblo*, 1920, J.R. Willis

40. *Julia Roybal and Alice Martinez Baking Bread*, 1974, M. K. Keegan

41. *Taos Pueblo*, photographer and date unknown

42. *Taos Pueblo*, 1970, M. K. Keegan

43. *Acoma Farmer*, 1892, Charles Lummis

44. *Farmers from Taos Pueblo,* 1969, M. K. Keegan

45. *Replastering a Paguate House, Laguna Pueblo,* 1925, Edward S. Curtis

46. *Replastering an Adobe House, Taos Pueblo*, 1969, M. K. Keegan

47. *Rosalie Winnowing Corn, San Ildefonso Pueblo,* 1920, Odd Halseth

48. *Woman Winnowing Corn, San Juan Pueblo,* 1972, M. K. Keegan

49. *Taos Man*, photographer and date unknown

50. *Leandro Bernal of Taos Pueblo*, 1974, M. K. Keegan

51. *San Juan Woman*, photographer and date unknown

52. *Geronima Archuleta from San Juan Pueblo*, 1980, M. K. Keegan

53. *Hopi Hairdressing*, 1901, Adam Clark Vroman

54. *Navajo Woman Combing Hair,* 1972, M. K. Keegan

55. *Cottonwood Tree at San Ildefonso Pueblo*, 1903, George H. Pepper

56. *Cottonwood Tree at San Ildefonso Pueblo*, 1987, M. K. Keegan

57. *Corn Dance, Jemez Pueblo*, photographer and date unknown

58. *Corn Dance, San Ildefonso Pueblo*, 1979, M. K. Keegan

59. *Deer Dance, San Ildefonso Pueblo*, January 23, 1920, Wesley Bradfield

60. *Deer Dance, San Ildefonso Pueblo*, January 23, 1973, M. K. Keegan

61. *Green Corn Dancers, Cochiti Pueblo,* 1935, T. Harmon Parkhurst

62. *The Peter Garcia Family, San Juan Pueblo*, 1980, M. K. Keegan

63. *Zuni Girl,* 1903, Edward S. Curtis

64. *Jutta Cajero from Jemez Pueblo*, 1986, M. K. Keegan

65. *Making Fry Bread, Taos Pueblo*, 1935, T. Harmon Parkhurst

66. *Christine and Bernadette Eustace from Zuni Pueblo Making Fry Bread*, 1978, M. K. Keegan

67. *The Potter, Santa Clara Pueblo*, 1905, Edward S. Curtis

68. *Rose Naranjo Making Pottery, Santa Clara Pueblo*, 1980, M. K. Keegan

69. *Firing Pottery, San Juan Pueblo,* photographer and date unknown

70. *Lucy and Richard Martinez Firing Pottery, San Ildefonso Pueblo*, 1972, M. K. Keegan

71. *Mohave*, 1903, Edward S. Curtis

72. *Dancer from Nambe Pueblo*, 1972, M. K. Keegan

73. *Apache Mountain Spirit Dancer*, date unknown, John K. Hillers

74. *Apache Mountain Spirit Dancer*, 1976, M. K. Keegan

75. *Navajo Hogan, Canyon de Chelly*, 1890, Ben Wittick

76. *Navajo Hogan, Monument Valley,* 1972, M. K. Keegan

77. *Dorothy Aguilar, San Ildefonso Pueblo,* 1935, T. Harmon Parkhurst

78. *Darlene Martinez, San Ildefonso Pueblo*, 1988, M. K. Keegan

79. *Three Horses*, 1905, Edward S. Curtis

80. *Dixon Palmer, Kiowa Indian*, 1978, M. K. Keegan

81. *Tablita Dancers and Singers, San Ildefonso Pueblo,* 1905, Edward S. Curtis

82. *Dancers and Drummers, San Ildefonso Pueblo*, 1974, M. K. Keegan

83. *Comanche Dance*, 1920, Odd Halseth

84. *Comanche Dance, San Ildefonso Pueblo*, 1974, M. K. Keegan

85. *Corn Dance, Santa Clara Pueblo*, 1911, Matilda Coxe Stevenson

86. *Corn Dance, San Juan Pueblo,* 1974, M. K. Keegan

87. *Zuni Rain Dance*, 1899, Adam Clark Vroman

88. *End of Corn Dance, Santa Clara Pueblo,* 1989, M. K. Keegan

THE FRONTIER PHOTOGRAPHERS

WESLEY BRADFIELD (1876–1929)

Wesley Bradfield was an archaeologist who practiced photography as an adjunct to his scientific work. Born in Michigan in 1876, he moved to Santa Fe in 1909, where he worked at the Museum of New Mexico and School of American Research.

He was noted for research into the Mimbres culture and served for a brief period during 1926 and 1927 as Associate Director of the San Diego Museum in California. At the time of his death in 1929, he had returned to Santa Fe to live. An obituary called him "one of the most expert photographers in the scientific field."

EDWARD S. CURTIS (1868–1952)

The best-known and most controversial of all early photographers of Indians, Curtis was born in rural Wisconsin in 1868. During his early years as a commercial photographer, he became renowned for his romantic landscapes and portraits. He included Indians in some early landscapes and photographed more when he accompanied an expedition to Alaska in 1899. By the next year, he had begun his project of recording on glass plates and in essays, portraits of all the surviving Indian peoples of North America. Optimistically, he estimated that the project would take ten years to complete.

His first expeditions, to Montana and the Southwest, were followed by more extended sojourns in the Northwest, Southwest, and Great Plains. He carried with him an elaborate photographic setup: a portable studio, darkroom, photo assistants, and even articles of traditional Indian dress and decoration to be used when sitters were unable to provide their own.

Diligent fund-raising was required to support this grand undertaking, and Curtis was helped in this when he met President Theodore Roosevelt. Roosevelt's enthusiastic support for Curtis's project helped raise money and was good for public relations; but Curtis's chief financial coup was in persuading J. Pierpont Morgan to become his backer. Morgan's capital, which permitted publication of the first volume of *The North American Indian* in 1907, continued to support Curtis's activities for some time. After Morgan's death in 1913, his son renewed the family's commitment to Curtis's project. Even with this assistance, the project continued to be time consuming, and was finally completed only in 1930 with the publication of volume 30 of *The North American Indian*.

The special qualities of Curtis's work derive in part from his deep sympathy with his subjects. It is said that he spent many hours sitting with them and passing the pipe while discussing their religious mysteries. Curtis himself had a gloomy view of the future of this culture, and wrote: *Alone with my campfire, I gaze about on the completely circling hilltop, crested with countless campfires, around which are gathered the people of a dying race. The gloom of the approaching night wraps itself about me. I feel that the life of these children of nature is like the dying day drawing to its end; only off in the West is the glorious light of the setting sun, telling us, perhaps, of light after darkness.* (1805)

Though immensely popular in his early life, Curtis's work fell into obscurity after 1930. Curtis became depressed and produced little after this time; he died in Los Angeles in 1952. Within a decade, in the 1960s and 1970s, the rediscovery of Curtis began. His work has since been celebrated and popularized to such an extent that he has become one of the best-known photographers of all time.

Many adoring, critical, or ambivalent essays have been written about Curtis's work. Some critics call his pictures contrived because he usually posed his subjects and sometimes costumed them as well. Others revere his photographs as a revelation of the nobility, glory, and moral superiority of Native American culture. Even if we criticize Curtis's pictures as ethnography, we have to appreciate them as art. Ethnographic research was rather new in Curtis's time, and standards for its practice were not rigorously defined. Standards of art, though constantly evolving, have been with us for a very long time, and are probably a more reliable means of assessing work as singular—and as irreplaceable—as Curtis's. Since *The North American Indian* is the only work of its kind, we can be grateful that it was made by an artist.

WYATT DAVIS (1906–1985)

As a photographer for the New Mexico State Tourist Bureau in the 1930s and 1940s, Wyatt Davis traveled to all parts of the state photographing Indians and other aspects of New Mexico culture for use in the bureau's major tourism promotions. Between 1936 and 1944, he made thousands of negatives, capturing the first photographs of New Mexico which were widely circulated through national advertising and travel articles. Born in East Orange, New Jersey, on February 14, 1906, Davis first visited New Mexico in the summer of 1923 at the age of seventeen. On this trip he accompanied his older brother, artist Stuart Davis, to Santa Fe, where they were guests of the noted artist John Sloan. Wyatt became intrigued with New Mexico during this first visit, and was determined to return after he had completed his education.

He was graduated from high school in New York, attended Columbia College for one year, and held various jobs in New York from 1926 to 1932. Returning to Santa Fe, he established a home and became a freelance photographer. Soon afterwards, he was employed by Joe Bursey, director of the New Mexico State Tourist Bureau (now the New Mexico Economic Development and Tourism Department), to photograph the state. Carrying a heavy view camera, he photographed extensively when weather permitted, developing his negatives during the winter months, often at the rate of eighty to one hundred per day. Some of his photographs are still used in travel articles. Davis left Santa Fe in the 1970s and moved to Oaxaca, Mexico. He died in 1985. (Biographical information courtesy of Byron Johnson, History Curator, Albuquerque Museum.)

BURTON FRASHER (1888–1955)

Burton Frasher, born in Denver, Colorado, on July 25, 1888, first became interested in photography as a boy in Colorado. As a young man, however, he moved to California to pursue a career making fruit packing boxes. As a box maker, he traveled throughout California and other western states where fruit was being harvested.

During these business trips, he began photographing again, carrying a large camera with him to photograph subjects of personal concern. This led to an interest in portrait photography, and in 1914 he opened his own photography studio in Pomona, California, and entered the postcard business, making use of his own images. By the late 1920s, the "Frasher Fotos" trademark was well established, and his images appeared on postcards and as guidebook illustrations. By 1930, he was photographing Indians in New Mexico and Arizona.

Frasher was best known as a desert photographer, spending considerable time in California's Death Valley. For his work he preferred oversize Crown cameras, some producing 7″x 17″ negatives. Frasher died in 1955, but his photography and postcard business continued to be operated by the family. In 1948 alone, the Frashers sold more than three million postcards.

ODD S. HALSETH (1894–1966)

Odd S. Halseth emigrated from Norway to America in his early twenties. An archaeologist, he found employment at the Museum of New Mexico and School of American Research in the 1920s. He was involved with the restoration of Zia Pueblo Mission and with excavations at Gran Quivira and Puye. In 1927, he moved to Phoenix, Arizona, where he served as City Archaeologist from 1927 to 1960. During that time he photographed the Southwestern Indian tribes. His wife, Edna Scofield, achieved recognition as a sculptor of Indian subjects.

JOHN K. HILLERS (1843–1925)

A German immigrant who had served in the Civil War and worked as a policeman in Brooklyn, John Hillers signed up as a boatman on John Wesley Powell's famous 1871 geological survey of the Grand Canyon and the Southwest. When Hillers saved Powell from drowning, the two men formed a lasting friendship.

Although he had no photographic training, Hillers volunteered to assist the expedition's photographer. He displayed great aptitude, and, when the chief photographer quit, Hillers quickly began making photographs himself. During Powell's next expedition the following year, Hillers had the job of chief photographer. It was the beginning of a twenty-nine-year career.

When Powell became the head of the United States Geological Survey in 1880, Hillers continued to work for him, making both geological and ethnographic photographs. On later expeditions, Powell sometimes asked Hillers's photographic subjects to wear items of Indian dress he provided from his own collection.

Hillers's work, often executed on plates at least 11″ x 14″, and sometimes as large as 28″ x 34″, is known for its sensitivity and technical mastery. During his career, he visited New Mexico and Arizona frequently, and devoted much time to photographing the Hopi and Pueblo people. He is credited with having over twenty-three thousand surviving negatives.

CHARLES FLETCHER LUMMIS (1859–1928)

Born in Lynn, Massachusetts, and educated at Harvard, Lummis learned the printing trade and rose quickly in the profession, becoming City Editor of the *Los Angeles Daily Times* by the age of twenty-six. His interest in photography probably developed as an adjunct to journalism. After covering the Apache wars in Arizona in 1886, Lummis suffered a paralyzing stroke. He moved to Isleta Pueblo in 1888, where he began seriously to photograph the Southwestern Indians and their culture, concentrating particularly on ceremonies and rituals.

In 1892, he accompanied Adolph Bandelier to South America, where he made many photographs in Peru. On his return, he founded the magazine *Out West* (originally *The Land of Sunshine*), which he edited until 1909. He devoted his energies to the preservation and interpretation of Southwestern Indian cultures.

Lummis published several books and many articles illustrated with his and others' photographs of Indians (including the photographs of Adam Clark Vroman). He was also a founder of the Southwest Museum in Los Angeles, California.

T. HARMON PARKHURST (1883–1952)

Like many other photographers of the period, Parkhurst also began his career in archaeology. Born in Middletown, New York, and educated at Oneonta and at Syracuse, Parkhurst first journeyed to Santa Fe as part of an archaeological expedition to Frijoles Canyon (now Bandelier National Monument). He stayed in the Southwest to work at the newly-founded Museum of New Mexico, where archaeologist Jesse Nusbaum served as museum photographer.

Parkhurst's early work with 5″ x 7″ glass plates reflects the training and influence of Nusbaum. In 1915, Parkhurst opened his own studio in Santa Fe and began enlarging and painting on photographic prints; he began using a 7″ x 11″ camera in the 1920s. Parkhurst photographed in Santa Fe, at the pueblos, and in the Spanish towns of northern New Mexico, producing many scenic views and regional portraits. His huge enlargements, over-painted by Indian artists such as the Navajo Quincy Tahoma, became popular collectibles for tourists. Parkhurst worked somewhat with color slides in his later years.

GEORGE HUBBARD PEPPER (1873–1924)

Pepper became interested in archaeology in childhood when he explored Indian sites near his home on Staten Island, New York. He studied at the Peabody Museum at Harvard University and received an appointment in 1896 as Assistant Curator in the Department of the Southwest at the American Museum of Natural History in New York.

He undertook expeditions in the Southwest which focused on Chaco Canyon, the occupied pueblos, and on researching Navajo textiles. In 1904, he met George G. Heye, under whose auspices he joined digs in Mexico and Ecuador. Pepper eventually served as Acting Curator of Heye's Museum of the American Indian in New York.

SIMEON SCHWEMBERGER (1867–1931)

Born in Cincinnati, Ohio, Schwemberger was baptized George Charles; he became a Franciscan Brother in 1896 and was given the name Simeon. In 1901, Brother Simeon Schwemberger went to St.Michael Franciscan Mission near Window Rock, Arizona, the headquarters for the Navajo Nation. He photographed Indians in the Southwest while he was at the mission and did most of his photography from 1901 to 1909.

In 1909, he left the mission and opened a photography shop in Gallup, New Mexico, which he managed for one year. The following year he worked for Hubbell at a trading post near Hopi, and in 1916 he opened his own trading post in Gallup, which he operated until his death.

MATILDA COXE STEVENSON (1850–1915)

A noted early ethnologist, Matilda Coxe Stevenson was married to James Stevenson, who worked for a geologist leading survey expeditions to the West. Both the Stevensons were photographers, and both were involved in the founding of the Bureau of Ethnology under John Wesley Powell in 1879.

Among others who traveled with the Stevensons was the great photographer William Henry Jackson. In fact, Jackson sold his camera equipment to his friend Stevenson for two hundred dollars when he retired in 1878.

After her husband's death in the mid-1880s, Matilda Coxe Stevenson continued her research and photography on her own, concentrating particularly on the Zia and Zuni Pueblos of New Mexico. Although she had initially been motivated by a desire to bring European "civilization" to the Indians, she eventually developed a genuine appreciation of native cultures after studying Indian language and religion. "Tilly" Stevenson was accepted into Indian society, and became one of the first government anthropologists to advocate the preservation of Native American culture.

ADAM CLARK VROMAN (1856–1916)

Born in Illinois, Vroman worked for a railroad for a time, then settled in Pasadena, California, where he opened a bookstore. Though he remained based in California for the rest of his life, Vroman found time to travel widely; he visited the Southwest many times and also made trips to Europe and the Orient, photographing wherever he went.

During his first trip to the Southwest in 1895, he went to the Hopi town of Walpi, where he photographed the Snake Dances. He also visited Navajo and other New Mexico pueblos—Zuni, Laguna, and Acoma. At Laguna Pueblo in 1897 he met Frederick Webb Hodge, who was then head of the Bureau of American Ethnology. Hodge invited Vroman to accompany him on the first expedition to climb Katzimo (Enchanted Mesa). This expedition was organized to find proof of the legend that the people of Acoma had once lived on top of this inaccessible mesa. Vroman made the ascent and took photographs of Indian ruins that proved, incontrovertibly, that human habitation had once existed there.

At his home in Pasadena, Vroman started a camera club which later organized expeditions for members to Hopi and other pueblos. He traveled again for F. W. Hodge, documenting the Rio Grande pueblos.

Vroman worked during a time when tourist travel to the pueblos was increasing and the Indians were growing wary of photographers. Indians began to ban or strictly control photography of their dances and sacred rites, but Vroman made the best of it. He was possibly among the last photographers to record some of the sacred dances. By 1911, photography was banned at all the Hopi villages, and Vroman directed his attention elsewhere, visiting the Orient, Hawaii, and the Canadian Rockies, among other places.

During his lifetime, Vroman's pictures sold widely to collectors and were published in magazines. After his death, his work vanished from the public eye until the 1950s when his entire collection was rediscovered and restored to public appreciation.

J. R. WILLIS (1876–1960)

Born in Sylvania, Georgia, Willis was educated at the New York School of Art. He worked in a tremendous variety of media, including newspaper cartoons, magazine illustrations, film cartoon animation, pastels, oil and watercolor paintings, and etchings. At some time during his career he also managed to spend ten years in vaudeville.

Willis did his first photographic work around the Navajo reservation and Canyon de Chelly beginning in 1903. By 1917, and especially during the 1920s, he was constantly traveling throughout the Southwest, spending much of his time on Indian reservations. He both photographed and painted, concentrating on landscapes and Indian subjects; he also produced photographic postcards, and painted murals in Albuquerque restaurants and Gallup schools.

GEORGE BEN WITTICK (1845–1903)

Born in Pennsylvania, Wittick first traveled to the West as a result of Army service at Fort Snelling, Minnesota. For a time he settled in Moline, Illinois, where he operated a photography studio. By 1878, he had moved to Santa Fe as a photographer for the Atchison, Topeka, and Santa Fe Railroad. He eventually opened a studio of his own there, moving later to Albuquerque and finally settling in Gallup and at Fort Wingate.

Throughout the 1880s he traveled across Arizona and New Mexico. He photographed Hopi Snake Dances at Walpi, Mishongnovi, and Oraibi, and visited and photographed Zuni as well. Along with John Hillers, he accompanied the Stevenson Expedition to Mummy Cave and into Canyon de Chelly.

Wittick died in 1903 at Fort Wingate, New Mexico, after being bitten by a rattlesnake he had captured as a gift for a Hopi Snake Dance.

PLATE INFORMATION

1. *Canyon de Chelly*, Edward S. Curtis, 1904. (Courtesy Museum of New Mexico, Negative No. 148663.)
From Curtis's own writings: *A wonderfully scenic spot is this in northeastern Arizona, in the heart of Navaho country—one of their strongholds, in fact. Canyon de Chelly exhibits evidences of having been occupied by a considerable number of people in former times, as in every niche at every side are seen the cliff-perched ruins of former villages. In Canyon de Chelly, which may be termed the garden spot of the reservation, there are diminutive farms and splendid peach orchards irrigated with fresh water.*

2. *Canyon de Chelly*, M. K. Keegan, 1972.
The horses in this photo were part of a Navajo wagon train that stretched beyond the frame of the picture. The family leading the horses was probably one of those that has lived in the canyon for generations.

The romantic landscape of Canyon de Chelly is one of the most celebrated in the Southwest. Dramatic rocks pierce vast skies, creating vistas in which individual man is insignificant, yet engulfed by beauty. Though I have photographed in the canyon for many years, in every season, one experience stands out. In 1959, I was sitting on the rim of the canyon at sunset when a Navajo on horseback rode down into the canyon singing a Navajo love song. He did not know anyone was listening, but the song that echoed throughout the canyon still echoes in my heart.

Scott Momaday, the Kiowa writer who wrote the foreword for this book, grew up among the Navajo. He remembers: *If you have ever been to the hogans in Canyon de Chelly, or to a Squaw Dance near Lukachukai— if you have ever heard the riding songs in the dusk, or the music of the Yeibichai (a Navajo healing ceremony)— you will never come away entirely, but a part of you will remain there always; you will have found an old home of the spirit.*

3. *Laguna Pueblo*, Ben Wittick, 1885. (Courtesy Museum of New Mexico, Negative No. 16052.)

4. *Laguna Pueblo*, M. K. Keegan, 1972.
Laguna Pueblo with its seven villages is located alongside Interstate 40, about forty miles west of Albuquerque, New Mexico. Archaeologists believe that the pueblo's first occupation dates from the mid-fifteenth century. Its ancient and celebrated mission, San Jose de Laguna, was founded in 1699.

5. *Acoma Woman at Waterhole*, Edward S. Curtis, 1904. (Courtesy Museum of New Mexico, Negative No. 76958.)
Acoma is situated atop a 357-foot-high sandstone mesa about sixty miles west of Albuquerque, New Mexico. Believed to be at least a thousand years old, the "Sky City," as it is sometimes called, is the oldest continuously inhabited community in the United States.

6. *Acoma Woman at Waterhole*, M. K. Keegan, 1970.
Curtis photographed women with pots, but the woman I photographed used a bucket which she then persuaded me to carry, for her, back up the wall to the mesa. The water at Acoma is still pure and wonderfully sweet to drink. One climbs down to the water basin via footholes in the side of the mesa. The footholes were designed for small feet and are hard to negotiate if your feet, like mine, are large.

7. *Caroline Trujillo, Cochiti Pueblo*, T. Harmon Parkhurst, 1920. (Courtesy Museum of New Mexico, Negative No. 2326.)

Near Interstate 25 between Santa Fe and Albuquerque, Cochiti Pueblo dates from the thirteenth century. Present-day Cochitis are the descendants of the ancient cliff dwellers at Bandelier, and still hold sacred rituals in the hills of their forefathers.

8. *Trina Encino from Acoma Pueblo*, M.K. Keegan, 1974.

When I found Caroline Trujillo's photograph, I was startled by the similarities between her image and that of a woman I had photographed more than fifty years later. Both Acoma and Cochiti are well known for their pottery. Cochiti potters specialize in black-and-white designs that often include animal shapes, and Acoma is famous for polychrome.

9. *Zuni Pueblo*, Edward S. Curtis, 1903. (Courtesy Museum of New Mexico, Negative No. 143701.)

This pueblo was probably the first to be seen by Europeans, when a Spanish expedition under the leadership of Coronado arrived here in 1540, in search of the mythical seven golden cities of Cibola. One of his soldiers gave us an early anthropological essay on Zuni social structure: *They do not have chiefs as in New Spain (Mexico), but are ruled by a council of the oldest men. They have priests, who preach to them, whom they call papas ("elder brothers"). These are the elders.... They tell them how they are to live, and I believe that they give certain commandments for them to keep, for there is no drunkenness among them nor sodomy nor sacrifices, neither do they eat human flesh nor steal, but they are usually at work....*

More than three hundred years later, in 1879, the celebrated archaeologist and anthropologist Frank Hamilton Cushing arrived at Zuni. Cushing was ultimately to be initiated as a priest of the bow, and his sympathetic attachment to the Zuni may be seen in his description of his first sight of the pueblo: *A banner of smoke, as though fed from a thousand crater-fires, balanced over this seeming volcano, floating off, in many a circle and surge, on the evening breeze. But I did not realize that this hill, so strange and picturesque, was a city of the habitation of man, until I saw, on the topmost terrace, little specks of black and red moving about against the sky.... Imagine numberless long, box-like shapes, adobe ranches, connected with one another in extended rows and squares, with others, less and less numerous, piled upon them lengthwise and crosswise, in two, three, even six stories, each receding from the one below it like the steps of a broken stair-flight— as if it were a gigantic pyramidal mud honeycomb with far outstretching base—and you can imagine a fair conception of the architecture of Zuni.*

10. *Taos Pueblo*, M.K. Keegan, 1969.

Although Zuni Pueblo has by now lost some of the many-layered upper stories it had in Cushing's day, Taos Pueblo still has many multi-story communal buildings, and retains more of the old look of the "pyramidal mud honeycomb." Its adobe cubes rise against the backdrop of thirteen thousand-foot-high Wheeler Peak, New Mexico's loftiest mountain.

11. *Corn Dance, Jemez Pueblo*, Simeon Schwemberger, 1908. (Courtesy Library of Congress.)

The dancers carry gourd rattles which they shake to attract rain; the sound is meant to imitate that of rain beating on the ground. This ceremony is meant to harmonize the critical elements of the natural environment that promote the growth of corn.

12. *Corn Dance, Santa Clara Pueblo*, M.K. Keegan, 1986.
The gourd rattles are prominent in the hands of the dancers; also visible are the spruce boughs that, along with the gourds, are meant to bring rain and fertility. The idea of increase in the corn crop carries with it, in this ceremony, overtones of human increase as well.

The use of certain significant implements and gestures; the movement of the dancers; their preparation and adornment—all are critical in enabling the Corn Dance to bring about fruitfulness and harmony in nature. Yet none of these things would be useful unless the dancers maintain the proper mental and emotional attitude.

Just as in ritual, a fragile ecological balance between man and nature is easily disturbed. Care and concentrated attention are required to husband the sparse water and to guard the crop and seed corn from mishap. It is easy to wreck the balance, to drive the Corn Maidens away—and far harder to restore it.

13. *Hopi Girl*, Edward S. Curtis, 1904. (Courtesy Library of Congress.)
Curtis captioned this photo of a young girl with her hair in the "squash blossom" style, "Primitive Style of Hairdressing."

14. *Hopi Girl*, M.K. Keegan, 1987.
I prefer to call my photo "Sophisticated Hairdressing"—thinking of the elaborately moussed and gelled twists seen on some very elegant big city women. The Hopi used U-shaped sticks called *gnelas* for shape, and squash seed oil for stiffness to create these "wheels," which symbolize squash blossoms, symbols of fertility. The style has been worn by unmarried Hopi women apparently for eons, to judge from reports of pictographs showing females with this characteristic hairstyle.

15. *Man from Taos Pueblo*, T. Harmon Parkhurst, 1935. (Courtesy Museum of New Mexico, Negative No. 22696.)

16. *Frank C. Romero from Taos Pueblo*, M.K. Keegan, 1970.
Wearing a blanket over the head is a natural way to keep out glare, sun, and cold—whatever excesses nature sends in a desert climate; and an adobe wall makes a perfect backdrop. Still, imagine my surprise, when, looking through Parkhurst's work for the first time in 1989, I came across his photograph so much like one I had taken thirty-seven years later. And I fully expect another photographer, in 2001, to see the same scene at Taos Pueblo and, unknowingly, take this same photograph again!

17. *Buffalo Herd*, Edward S. Curtis, 1905. (Courtesy Museum of New Mexico, Negative No. 148665.)

18. *Buffalo Herd, Taos Pueblo*, M.K. Keegan, 1970.

The deliberate, nearly total eradication of buffalo from the plains is one of the saddest stories of the West. But buffalo have been on the increase in places like reservations and national parks where they are permitted to graze. On the Taos reservation, where the Indians maintain their own herd, one can see groups of the great shaggy creatures scattered across the prairie, and imagine the vast herds that once thundered throughout central North America.

19. *Buffalo Dancers, Tesuque Pueblo*, Edward S. Curtis, 1925. (Courtesy Museum of New Mexico, Negative No. 144657.)

20. *Buffalo Dancers, Nambe Pueblo*, M.K. Keegan, 1969.

21. *Buffalo Dance, San Ildefonso Pueblo*, Wesley Bradfield, 1920. (Courtesy Museum of New Mexico, Negative No. 82160.)

22. *Buffalo Dance, San Ildefonso Pueblo*, M.K. Keegan, 1973.
The Buffalo Dance, usually held in the winter months, is a celebration of the creature whose life was once so intertwined with that of the Indians. During the dance, the presence of the buffalo is invoked; he is honored for laying down his life for mankind and prayers are made for his return. When the buffalo is symbolically "shot" by the Indians, his spirit goes forth to report on the behavior of the tribe. A favorable report assures another year of cooperation between the buffalo spirit and the Indian tribe.

Vincent Scully described a Buffalo Dance which he witnessed in 1968. It had only one girl dancer. He was particularly impressed with her grace and compassion when, with a final gesture, she closed the dance by blessing (and condemning) the buffalo by laying her sacred bouquet on its head with exquisite tenderness. With that gesture he experienced a summary of the buffalo's continuous cycle of death and rebirth. To Scully, this invocation of the cycles of nature corresponded to other cultures' mythical images, such as those of Artemis and Athena, and suggested for him a pantheon of divine beings governing the natural laws.

23. *Dancer with Tablita*, Edward S. Curtis, 1905. (Courtesy Museum of New Mexico, Negative No. 144546.)

24. *Bernice Roybal from San Ildefonso Pueblo*, M.K. Keegan, 1980.
Bernice in her *tablita* (a symbol of clouds) could be the cheerful, contemporary sister of the young woman Curtis photographed seventy-five years before. Bernice is dressed in the *manta*, the traditional black, one-shouldered dance dress. Pueblo women have been wearing clothing woven of cotton cloth since pre-Columbian times. The *manta* is one-shouldered because it is supposed to be open on the side next to the heart. When women die, they are buried in their *mantas*, reversed so that the right shoulder is exposed, rather than the left. Also, after death the moccasins are reversed, with the right shoe on the left foot and vice versa.

I have known Bernice since she was a child, and have photographed her over the years. An early photo of Bernice, standing on the kiva steps at San Ildefonso Pueblo, appears as Plate 32. One of her three children, Darlene, is shown in Plate 78.

25. *Acoma Pueblo*, Wyatt Davis, date unknown. (Courtesy Museum of New Mexico, Negative No. 58317.)
Acoma's name is derived from the Keresan (Pueblo language) word *akoma* (people of the white rock), a name which refers to the butte on which the pueblo sits.

26. *Acoma Pueblo*, M.K. Keegan, 1972.
When Wyatt Davis photographed Acoma, it was nearly deserted. Its recorded population in 1850 was only three hundred and fifty people. By the end of the 1980s, Acoma Pueblo and its outlying community had a population of over three thousand people. Like the other pueblos, Acoma's growth can be ascribed to an increase in the birth rate, extended longevity, and the fact that more people are choosing not to leave the reservation.

27. *Making Pottery, Santa Clara Pueblo*, Burton Frasher, 1920. (Courtesy Museum of New Mexico, Negative No. 134717.)
Pottery-making is an ancient art in the Southwest. Almost every American museum visitor has seen centuries-old Indian pots whose form and decoration rank with the finest made anywhere in the world.

Santa Clara has long been celebrated for its pottery, which includes glazed red-and-black as well as multi-colored designs. Designs and techniques are handed down through families, and, according to anthropologist Ruth Bunzel, there are no rules of proportion. In the 1920s, she quoted an Indian potter as saying, by way of general principles, *It must be even all around, not larger on one side than another. We must therefore believe the potter,* said Bunzel, *when she said, 'I carry all the designs in my head and never get them mixed up.'*

28. *Lucy Martinez, San Ildefonso Pueblo*, M.K. Keegan, 1972.
The pottery of San Ildefonso has brought it international renown. In the 1920s, Maria Martinez and her husband Julian brought about a resurgence in the craft of blackware pottery in which the design is formed by contrasting elements of matte black and highly polished black. Other pottery produced at San Ildefonso includes the perhaps more traditional redware and polychrome.

Lucy Martinez and her husband Richard (a relative of Maria Martinez) were married for over sixty years and worked together the entire time. Lucy formed the pots and he decorated them.

29. *"The Estufa"* [Kiva], *San Ildefonso Pueblo*, Edward S. Curtis, 1905. (Courtesy Museum of New Mexico, Negative No. 144541.)
Estufa is the old word for kiva, the underground chamber where religious ceremonies are held, and where dancers go to prepare for the sacred dances. They are holy places, and closed to everyone but pueblo members.

30. *Dancers Entering Kiva, Nambe Pueblo*, M.K. Keegan, 1971.
The most recognizable kivas are the round, above-ground structures entered through the roof—like those pictured at San Ildefonso and at Nambe—but kivas may also be rectangular. In the round ones we may recognize traces of the creation myths common to Pueblos—of man emerging into this world through a hole in the ground. By going down into the round kiva through the hole in the roof, the Indian is going back into unity

with Mother Earth, into the womb of his creation before the separation from the Divine took place.

In this kiva the dancer becomes consecrated, charged with the energy of the being or force he is to represent in the dance. When he or she emerges from the kiva, it is really the spirit of the totemic creature that appears.

31. *Estufa* [Kiva], *San Ildefonso Pueblo*, George H. Pepper, 1904. (Courtesy Museum of the American Indian, Negative No. 2494.)

32. *Bernice at Kiva, San Ildefonso Pueblo*, M.K. Keegan, 1971.
The kiva in Pepper's photograph looks so lonely and deserted, but as the presence of young Bernice suggests in my photograph, the young people are returning to the kivas and to the sacred festivals in general.

In most pueblos, the people are divided into two groups, the "summer people" and the "winter people," each of which has a chief. The "summer" chief rules during the growing season and harvest, and the "winter" chief rules during the colder months. This, at least, seems to have been the traditional system, though modern acculturation has brought many changes, and hence variations on this basic system. Many pueblo villages have separate kivas for the "summer people" and the "winter people," and a third kiva where both may meet together. In some pueblos, like Taos, there are many kivas. Whether the old "summer people"/"winter people" system still holds true or not, the kivas in today's pueblos are much in use.

33. *Eagle Dance, Cochiti Pueblo*, T. Harmon Parkhurst, 1935. (Courtesy Museum of New Mexico, Negative No. 2258.)

34. *Eagle Dance, Laguna Pueblo*, M.K. Keegan, 1970.
Along with the resurgence in spiritual and social activity centered around traditional Pueblo life, Pueblo peoples have experienced a resurgence of desire for privacy, to protect the sacredness of their ceremonies. In the old days, many pueblos allowed photography or sketching of many of their dances and ritual objects that may no longer even be seen by non-Indians.

I was fortunate, in 1958, to see a Zuni Shalako Dance. It was one of the first experiences I had of Pueblo culture, and it made a life-long impression on me. In 1990, the Shalako Dance was closed to non-Indian attendance. There are some early photographs of the Shalako Dance (Hillers photographed it at Zuni in 1879), but no one has been allowed to photograph it during this century.

Similarly, though I was able to photograph the Eagle Dance pictured here in 1970, Eagle Dances may no longer be photographed by anyone. The emphasis is now on protecting the sacred atmosphere of the ceremony, rather than on documenting a belief system—which is quite certainly no longer vanishing.

35. *Little Daylight*, Edward S. Curtis, 1905. (Courtesy Library of Congress.)

36. *Kiowa Boy*, M.K. Keegan, 1978.
Because of Curtis's habit of occasionally pulling a traditional costume piece out of his own closet to replace the more modern clothes of his sitter, it is impossible to speculate on what Little Daylight might normally have

worn. But I can tell you that the Kiowa boy in my own photograph wears jeans, like any other boy in the United States. On ceremonial days, however, he wears his own traditional costume, pieces of which may have been made by him or handed down through generations.

37. *Hopi Basket Maker*, Adam Clark Vroman, 1901, Gates Expedition. (Courtesy Southwest Museum, Negative No. 22682.)

38. *Navajo Basket Makers*, M.K. Keegan, 1970.
Basket weaving, like pottery, was once practiced entirely for utilitarian purposes, and baskets were decorated with traditional motifs, often distinctive at each pueblo. There is an international decorative arts market for basketry that has, like the markets for pottery and jewelry, spurred the reclamation of this ancient craft. Since basket weaving is less remunerative and popular than pottery, it is practiced on a smaller scale—but it is still practiced. The baskets made are both traditional and innovative in design.

39. *Mrs. Yaweya Baking Bread in Horno, Laguna Pueblo*, J. R. Willis, 1920. (Courtesy Museum of New Mexico, Negative No. 42111.)

40. *Julia Roybal and Alice Martinez Baking Bread*, M.K. Keegan, 1974.
The horno, a traditional outdoor adobe oven, has been used for centuries. When they are very young, Pueblo daughters begin learning to make bread by practicing alongside their mothers. Agnes Dill, of Isleta Pueblo, recalled that her mother had three hornos, "a great big oven, and then a middle-sized oven called a family oven, and then she had one little tiny one for me."

41. *Taos Pueblo*, photographer and date unknown. (Courtesy Museum of the American Indian, Negative No. 35100.)

42. *Taos Pueblo*, M.K. Keegan, 1970.
The multi-story tiers of Taos may look as though they have been there forever, but in fact the town has been moved repeatedly. Though the present town has been there since the fifteenth century, ruins of several prehistoric foundations of the town have been identified. A series of archaeological sites reveals that Taos has moved gradually down out of the foothills of the mountains toward the plains.

The present pueblo is built in two principal units, North House and South House, that face each other across a stream known as the Taos River. The stream comes down from their sacred Blue Lake, on top of Taos Mountain, in the Sangre de Cristo mountain range. The Taos people make an annual pilgrimage to the sacred Blue Lake.

43. *Acoma Farmer*, Charles Lummis, 1892. (Courtesy Southwest Museum, Negative No. 22600.)
Even today, livestock and farming are principal sources of income on Acoma Pueblo.

44. *Farmers from Taos Pueblo*, M.K. Keegan, 1969.

The Taos farmers are, left to right, Thomas Martinez, Josecito Suazo, and Pat Suazo. Like Acoma, Taos has good grazing and farming lands which are still being used for agriculture. Although farmers use some modern techniques recommended for their particular crops and climate, they also still use ancient methods that were developed in this special environment and thus provide the best solutions for the problems it poses. The similarities in farmers' headgear pictured in 1892 and in 1969 may serve as an example.

45. *Replastering a Paguate House, Laguna Pueblo*, Edward S. Curtis, 1925. (Courtesy Museum of New Mexico, Negative No. 31961.)
Paguate is one of Laguna Pueblo's seven villages. The others are Mesita, Encinal, Paraja, Casa Blanca, Seama, and Laguna.

46. *Replastering an Adobe House, Taos Pueblo*, M.K. Keegan, 1969.
Adobe, or unbaked, sun-dried clay, has long been the traditional building material of the Pueblo people. Located further north and occupied at an earlier time, Mesa Verde might have been constructed of masonry; but here the buildings are heaped up from the earth with wet clay, lovingly smoothed by hand as though they were hand-turned pots for dwelling in. To understand the inspiration for these shapes, we have to look to the mountains that frame the pueblos or to the mesas against which they rise. The ancient adobe walls pay homage to the earth by using her materials and imitating her forms.

47. *Rosalie Winnowing Corn, San Ildefonso Pueblo*, Odd Halseth, 1920. (Courtesy Museum of New Mexico, Negative No. 32964.)

48. *Woman Winnowing Corn, San Juan Pueblo*, M.K. Keegan, 1972.
Corn was and is the principal Pueblo food, and every aspect of its growth and preparation is the occasion of some ritual or social activity. Morning prayers begin with the offering of cornmeal to the four directions. There are dances for green corn and for the harvest. Indian women grind corn to the singing of Indian men. Indians believe that their bodies are to some degree made up of corn, which is a reasonable belief in light of its dominance in the Indian diet.

49. *Taos Man*, photographer and date unknown. (Courtesy Museum of the American Indian, Negative No. 34732.)

50. *Leandro Bernal of Taos Pueblo*, M.K. Keegan, 1974.
Leandro Bernal lives a life today that is not vastly different from that of the unknown Taos man in the facing photograph (who might even have been an ancestor of Mr. Bernal). A maker of traditional moccasins, Bernal lives in the old portion of Taos Pueblo. He has neither electricity nor running water.

51. *San Juan Woman*, photographer and date unknown. (Courtesy Museum of the American Indian, Negative No. 35019.)

52. *Geronima Archuleta from San Juan Pueblo*, M.K. Keegan, 1980.

What strikes me most about the similarity between these two photographs goes beyond the surface likeness of appearance and style of dress; it has to do with the inner being that radiates from each of these women. They both seem poised and infinitely wise; they both are warm, but their human warmth is tempered by a stillness that emanates from the center of their beings.

Geronima's traditional nature is visible here; she normally wore Pueblo clothes and moccasins she made herself, and she was a potter and moccasin maker. Geronima died in 1990 at the age of eighty-five. Though the traditional clothes are still worn at dances, the younger Indians no longer wear them on a daily basis.

53. *Hopi Hairdressing*, Adam Clark Vroman, 1901. (Courtesy Southwest Museum, Negative No. 37162.)

This is one of a series of photographs Vroman made showing how the "squash blossom" hairstyle is achieved. By 1901, six years had passed since Vroman's first visit to the Hopi, and he had developed enough rapport with them to be permitted to move indoors with his cumbersome camera in order to document the details of daily life.

54. *Navajo Woman Combing Hair*, M.K. Keegan, 1972.

It is truly much simpler to use a 35mm camera and roll film, rather than glass plates, to record this sort of scene. Otherwise, the procedure has not changed much.

It is said that combing the hair with yucca is very good for the hair.

55. *Cottonwood Tree at San Ildefonso Pueblo*, George H. Pepper, 1903. (Courtesy Museum of the American Indian, Negative No. 32536.)

56. *Cottonwood Tree at San Ildefonso Pueblo*, M.K. Keegan, 1987.

When I discovered the Pepper photograph of this same cottonwood tree I had photographed eighty-four years later, I marvelled at how much that tree must have seen! How many dances has this great tree witnessed? How many private conversations and public ceremonies has it shaded? This tree has stood so long that the houses in Pepper's photograph are gone, and the plaza looks quite different today. Juan Cruz Bernal, a San Ildefonso Pueblo Indian who was born in 1895, remembered the tree being there, fully grown, when he was small. It is impossible to tell its exact age.

57. *Corn Dance, Jemez Pueblo*, photographer and date unknown. (Courtesy Library of Congress.)

58. *Corn Dance, San Ildefonso Pueblo*, M.K. Keegan, 1979.

The myths associated with the growth of corn involve the Sun God, his deputy Piayatiami, and the Corn Maidens. When their god-brother falls in love with them, the Corn Maidens flee. They must be coaxed and beseeched by Piayatiami to return, in order to provide continuing harvests for mankind. There are usually eight Corn Maidens — six for the corn of the colors of the six directions (north, south, east, west, above, and below); a seventh for sweet corn; and a final maiden for their companion, squash. Sometimes other maidens represent muskmelon or watermelon — making up a full spectrum of the staples of the Indian diet.

59. *Deer Dance, San Ildefonso Pueblo*, Wesley Bradfield, January 23, 1920. (Courtesy Museum of New Mexico, Negative No. 90120.)

60. *Deer Dance, San Ildefonso Pueblo*, M.K. Keegan, January 23, 1973.
At San Ildefonso's traditional feast day on January 23, both Buffalo and Deer Dances are performed. Like the Buffalo Dances, the Deer Dances are rituals of propitiation and thanksgiving, in which the Pueblos invoke and honor the spirit of the animal who dies in order that they may live. The "deer" come down the hill behind the pueblo at sunrise and dance all day. Though the Pueblos no longer depend on the deer or the buffalo for meat and clothing, the Indians believe that the dances still have value in harmonizing the forces of nature, on which we are all dependent for our well-being.

 This dance is traditionally held in December or January at various pueblos, and the date of the San Ildefonso dance has been consistent for many years. It is gratifying to note that there are at least as many dancers in my photo, made sixty-eight years later, as Bradfield saw in 1920.

61. *Green Corn Dancers, Cochiti Pueblo*, T. Harmon Parkhurst, 1935. (Courtesy Museum of New Mexico, Negative No. 2478.)

62. *The Peter Garcia Family, San Juan Pueblo*, M.K. Keegan, 1980.
The Garcia family, left to right, is: Peter Garcia, Sr., Peter Garcia, Jr., and Joe Garcia. The Garcia family and Parkhurst's *Green Corn Dancers* might have been photographed weeks apart, rather than years, considering the resemblances between them. The Garcia family is illustrative of the modern Indian's ability to blend tradition with active careers in the modern world. Peter Garcia, Sr., is a composer of traditional dance songs and is widely known through tape recordings of his songs and through performances of his dance company. His son, Peter Garcia, Jr., is a contractor, and Joe Garcia is a scientist at Los Alamos National Scientific Laboratory.

63. *Zuni Girl*, Edward S. Curtis, 1903. (Courtesy Museum of New Mexico, Negative No. 144735.)

64. *Joetta Cajero from Jemez Pueblo*, M.K. Keegan, 1986.
These two girls might be spiritual sisters, alike in beauty and in style of adornment, Joetta Cajero's beauty has, however, received official acclaim in the modern style. In 1986, this young woman was voted the winner of the Miss Indian Beauty Contest.

65. *Making Fry Bread, Taos Pueblo*, T. Harmon Parkhurst, 1935. (Courtesy Museum of New Mexico, Negative No. 4415.)

66. *Christine and Bernadette Eustace from Zuni Pueblo Making Fry Bread*, M.K. Keegan, 1978.
Traditional Indian fry bread is round and puffy from being fried in oil or lard over a fire. Eaten plain or used as the basis for Indian tacos, it has been a staple of the diet for a long time.

 The two sisters in my photograph call themselves Zuni-Cochiti because their mother was from Cochiti. Zuni Pueblo has long been famous for its jewelry, and both sisters are jewelers. Christine and Bernadette learned the ancient craft and use it to make non-traditional designs which are very popular.

67. *The Potter, Santa Clara Pueblo*, Edward S. Curtis, 1905. (Courtesy Museum of New Mexico, Negative No. 143722.)

68. *Rose Naranjo Making Pottery, Santa Clara Pueblo*, M.K. Keegan, 1980.
The pottery of Santa Clara is among the most celebrated of Pueblo crafts. The skills are handed down by parents to children, if the children are talented. Rose Naranjo, of Santa Clara, has six daughters and six grandchildren who are all potters. Her son, Michael, is celebrated as a sculptor in bronze, and her daughters Tessie, Jody, Edna, Dollie, Nora, and Louisa are all well-known potters.

69. *Firing Pottery, San Juan Pueblo*, photographer and date unknown. (Courtesy Museum of the American Indian, Negative No. 32475.)

70. *Lucy and Richard Martinez Firing Pottery, San Ildefonso Pueblo*, M.K. Keegan, 1972.
Lucy and her late husband Richard lived at San Ildefonso and worked together for sixty years making the blackware pottery that is traditional there. Their techniques for firing are probably very similar to those portrayed in the early photograph taken at San Juan Pueblo. Cedar and cow dung are used to fire the pottery. In the old days, buffalo dung would have been used.

71. *Mohave*, Edward S. Curtis, 1903. (Courtesy Museum of New Mexico, Negative No. 148664.)

72. *Dancer from Nambe Pueblo*, M.K. Keegan, 1972.
We have no clue to the activity for which the Mohave was dressed in Curtis's photograph—other than perhaps posing for Curtis's camera. The Nambe Indian I photographed in 1972 was dressed for the dance, and the intensity of concentration displayed might be attributed to ritual preparation or a serious sense of purpose. Both visages are strikingly in possession of a gravity that a nineteenth-century writer would certainly call "noble."

73. *Apache Mountain Spirit Dancer*, John K. Hillers, date unknown. (Courtesy Museum of New Mexico, Negative No. 57776.)

74. *Apache Mountain Spirit Dancer*, M.K. Keegan, 1976.
The Apache Mountain Spirits are benevolent beings that drive away evil spirits who cause misfortune.

75. *Navajo Hogan, Canyon de Chelly*, Ben Wittick, 1890. (Courtesy School of American Research Collection in the Museum of New Mexico, Negative No. 16285.)

76. *Navajo Hogan, Monument Valley*, M.K. Keegan, 1972.
The Navajo still build and live in hogans, which may be constructed of either wood or adobe. Some modern features may appear in these hogans—such as TV sets—but Indians still honor traditional customs as well. The door must face east, and the hogan must be entered by walking towards the left. In other words, technolo-

gies may come and go, but the important things remain the same.

77. *Dorothy Aguilar, San Ildefonso Pueblo*, T. Harmon Parkhurst, 1935. (Courtesy Museum of New Mexico, Negative No. 9217.)

78. *Darlene Martinez, San Ildefonso Pueblo*, M.K. Keegan, 1988.
Dorothy and Darlene, dressed for the dances, look like they could be preparing to attend the same ceremony, although they are actually three generations apart and Dorothy is Darlene's great aunt.

79. *Three Horses*, Edward S. Curtis, 1905. (Courtesy Library of Congress.)

80. *Dixon Palmer, Kiowa Indian*, M.K. Keegan, 1978.
Dixon Palmer, an Oklahoma Kiowa, is famous as a maker of traditional war bonnets. The beadwork he is wearing is typical of the styles traditional among Plains Indians. The resemblances between Dixon Palmer's and Three Horses's ornaments confirm that these ancient crafts are still alive.

81. *Tablita Dancers and Singers, San Ildefonso Pueblo*, Edward S. Curtis, 1905. (Courtesy Museum of New Mexico, Negative No. 144504.)

82. *Dancers and Drummers, San Ildefonso Pueblo*, M.K. Keegan, 1974.
In *Pueblo, Mountain Village Dance*, Vincent Scully described his impression of a Corn Dance: *[They] emerge toward noontime from one of the round kivas, women and men together. The men are stripped to the waist wearing only a white Hopi kilt and with lots of evergreen tied to their arms. They wear parrot feathers in their hair and skunk fur around their moccasin heels, and hold a rattle in one hand and evergreen in the other, with a turtleshell rattle gurgling away behind one knee. The women are in the traditional black dress, leaving one shoulder bare, hair generally long, feet bare, evergreen in each hand, the tablita, itself a stepped sky altar, on the head.*

83. *Comanche Dance*, Odd Halseth, 1920. (Courtesy Museum of the American Indian, Negative No. 32910.)

84. *Comanche Dance, San Ildefonso Pueblo*, M.K. Keegan, 1974.
The Pueblos often met with Comanches while hunting buffalo on Comanche territory. As a gesture of friendship, the Pueblos added this dance to their repertoire; it is a social dance. The Pueblos paint their bodies like war parties, and the women escort their warriors to the dance. It is performed in Comanche style with Pueblo adaptations.

85. *Corn Dance, Santa Clara Pueblo*, Matilda Coxe Stevenson, 1911. (Courtesy Smithsonian Institution, Negative No. 1982C.)

86. *Corn Dance, San Juan Pueblo*, M.K. Keegan, 1974.
Also in *Pueblo, Mountain Village Dance*, Vincent Scully observed, *Every Corn Dance has always seemed to me*

as much in praise of the power of the polis, almost as much military as agricultural in character.... Almost everybody seems to dance in it who can lift a foot. The plaza is never still. First one kiva dances, then the other, coiling around through it in a labyrinthian pattern, their banners passing each other as one group enters and one goes out. [When] they dance together...the whole plaza is one sea of evergreen and cloud altars, with drum beat and singing....

87. *Zuni Rain Dance*, Adam Clark Vroman, 1899. (Courtesy Seaver Center for Western History Research, Natural History Museum of Los Angeles County, Negative No. V–2352.)

88. *End of Corn Dance, Santa Clara Pueblo*, M.K. Keegan, 1989.
At the end of the Corn Dance, the dancers assemble on the roof of the kiva and return inside, to the sacred chamber, the center of the earth. All is made whole, all is harmony between heaven and earth. At the end of the twentieth century, all is yet well among the Pueblo Indians. We face the twenty-first century hoping that it will be a time when non-Indians begin more and more to understand the message of this profound culture, and to find ways to apply it to their own lives.